Feng Shui

Feng Shui for The Novice: Bring the Harmony and Energy of Feng Shui Into Your Household!

Table of Contents

Introduction

Picture yourself coming home from a long day to find a messy, cluttered house where your mismatched cushions clash with the wall behind them and your coffee table is overflowing with magazines, mail and ornaments. Now, picture yourself coming home from the same long day to a tidy, well organised house which exudes a feeling of calmness, peace and flow. Which would you prefer? If you answered the latter, keep reading for more information about feng shui and how it can help you.

The words Feng Shui literally translate to "wind" and "water". When taken together the term relates to balance, or harmony. When you practice feng shui you are allowing yourself to be in harmony with your surroundings. This creates a peaceful, healthy and productive environment for you to flourish in.

Feng shui is built in off the principle that everything has energy, and that it is beneficial for you to align this energy into a harmonious state. When this aligned state is achieved it can help to reduce stress, bring you good fortune, and even improve your love life.

The practice of feng shui extends to all elements your home or work life, including but not limited to; the colors of your walls, the positioning of your furniture, the decorations on your walls and shelves and the types of plants you have. Read on to find out more about the history of feng shui, and how feng shui can work for you.

So, before staring your journey in Feng Shui, let me express my gratitude to you for downloading this book and I really hope that it will help you.

Quick History of Feng Shui

Feng shui has its roots in many ancient philosophies including Taoism, Confucianism, Buddhism, Shinto and Vashtu Shastri. The origins of Feng Shui can be traced back more than 3,000 years to rural China. It is believed to have initially developed amongst peasants when they were deciding where to erect their homes, grow their crops, and, perhaps most importantly dig burial sites. Each of these functions was believed to require auspicious signs to find the correct placement.

For example, when choosing a place to set up a dwelling they would look for a nearby river, and frequently build a house facing the north meaning they would experience warm sun in winter and cool breezes in summertime. Meanwhile, when selecting a site for a grave they would select one which faced east to west, and bury their dead pointing to the west. According to the Yin and Yang theory east represents yang energy and new life, and the west represents yin energy and older life. What is now known as Feng shui eventually emerged from these processes.

During the nineteenth century, a man by the name of Yang Yun-sung, who is widely regarded as the Grand Master of Feng Shui began teaching the importance of what he called dragon's energy or dragons breathe. This involved careful examination of the shape of the surrounding land (mountains, hills and rivers) to find areas which were symbolic of auspicious animal shapes (dragons, tigers etc). He taught that within these areas were great concentrations of positive energy, also called Qi, which were beneficial to humans. This became known as the Form school of feng shui (also sometimes called the Landscape school).

A century or so later another feng shui school known as the Compass school emerged under the guidance of a man known as Wang Chih. The compass school sought to adopt the principles of feng shui in different, often flat landscapes. As its name suggests, this type of feng shui uses a compass, and also an instrument called a bagua or pakua. A bagua is simply a feng shui map of your space. The bagua has eight sections relating to each of the cardinal points (north, south, east, and west, northeast, southeast northwest, southeast and southwest). When used together the bagua and compass allow individuals to maximise the Qi in their environment.

The practice of feng shui has been gradually and consistently shaped through each generation of Chinese society. At one point the population of feng shui grew so great that entire cities were designed and constructed using its principles. However, practicing feng shui was discouraged and eventually supressed in China during the cultural revolution of the 1960s, but it has since found popularity in other countries. In recent times it has seen a revival in China and Hong Kong also.

During the 1990s feng shui gained widespread recognition through the Western world as part of a trend embracing many Eastern and New Age philosophies. In particular one school of feng shui known as the Black Sect Tantric Buddhist Feng Shui (BTB), gained immense popularity. This school was bought to the United States in the 1980s by Professor Thomas Lin Yun. Initially it had strong ties to Tibetan and Chinese Buddhism as well as Taoism and folk wisdom, though overtime it has gradually been increasingly adapted to suit the Western lifestyle thus losing some of its spiritual grounding.

How does it work?

One of the fundamental principles of feng shui to understand is that *everything has energy.* This also means that everything is connected through energy (including you). The practice of feng shui aligns this energy harmoniously so that it flows in a positive way allowing you to prosper in all aspects of your life. If there is too much, or too little energy harmony will not be achieved.

Yin and yang naturally flow in opposite directions, and neither can exist without the presence of the other (similar to light and darkness). Yin and yang are in a constant, never-ending state of flux - as one increases the other decreases. The practice of feng shui lies in finding a balance between the ying and yang in your life. In addition, there must be a harmony between the five elements of Qi (earth, fire, water, wood and metal).

Feng shui requires you to 'tune in' to the frequency of your surroundings. This includes your interior and exterior space, light, sounds, smells, materials and your furniture arrangement. As you tune in, you will become aware of your own energy and whether or not you are in balance with your surroundings. You may feel out of sync, slightly "off" in certain spaces. According to feng shui this discomfort is caused by an imbalance of energy. In order for harmony to be achieved, Qi must be able to flow uninhibited by negative energies.

Today, many feng shui experts combine the Form and Compass schools, and use them in combination with the principals of the Yin-Yang theory and the theory of Five Elements. These schools, and the Black Sect Tantric Buddhist school are commonly used in America and other Western countries. The BTB School also draws upon the Yin-Yang theory, and the five elements theory. Neither of these are better or worse, rather it is a matter of finding what works for you and your needs.

The practice of feng shui as outlined by the Form and Compass schools involves using a bagua (map of your living or work space) in conjunction with a compass to orient the optimal direction for certain purposes. A bagua is used to decide which aspects of the individual's life correspond to a specific space. The North direction represents your career, South - your reputation, East – health and family, West – creativity and children, Northeast – knowledge, Northwest – travel, Southeast – wealth, Southwest – love and relationships, and the centre which links each of the eight directions together. Each of these locations are also associated with a natural element (earth, water, fire, and wood, metal), a color and an animal.

The BTB School of feng shui also uses a bagua, although BTB focuses on the interior of a building and aligns the bagua with the entryway rather than a compass. Once the bagua is correctly oriented you can determine which room relates to which section. For instance, as the wall of your house including your front door is always aligned with the bottom of the bagua, it will be associated with one of these three areas; personal growth, your career or path in life, or, blessings. When you have determined which space relates to which specific area of your life, you can utilise feng shui to create harmony throughout.

There are many ways you can use feng shui to improve your life. Feng shui's principles can be applied to everything from choosing the location of a building to designing the layout of rooms in a house to the arrangement of items on your office desk. Creating harmony depends on the individual's needs, and their specific space. For instance, if you want to increase your creativity in your workspace, you could do one or more of the following things; add a wind chime to stimulate energy, place some living plants around – especially ones with white flowers, incorporate oval or circular items and hang some whimsical, fun art which reminds you of childhood, or which you find inspiring.

Another example is if you are having trouble sleeping. There are several things you can do to create a harmonious environment which will relax, and re-energise you. Some examples include removing electronic items such as televisions and computers as these interfere with the energy of the room. Opening the windows, or having an air purifier to ensure clean, oxygenated air is also important. The colors of the bedroom should be warm, skin tones such as cream, tan or chocolate brown. There should also be gentle light such as candles (toxic free candles), and all doors should be kept closed while you are sleeping to allow yourself to be nourished by the flow of energy within the room.

The Living Room

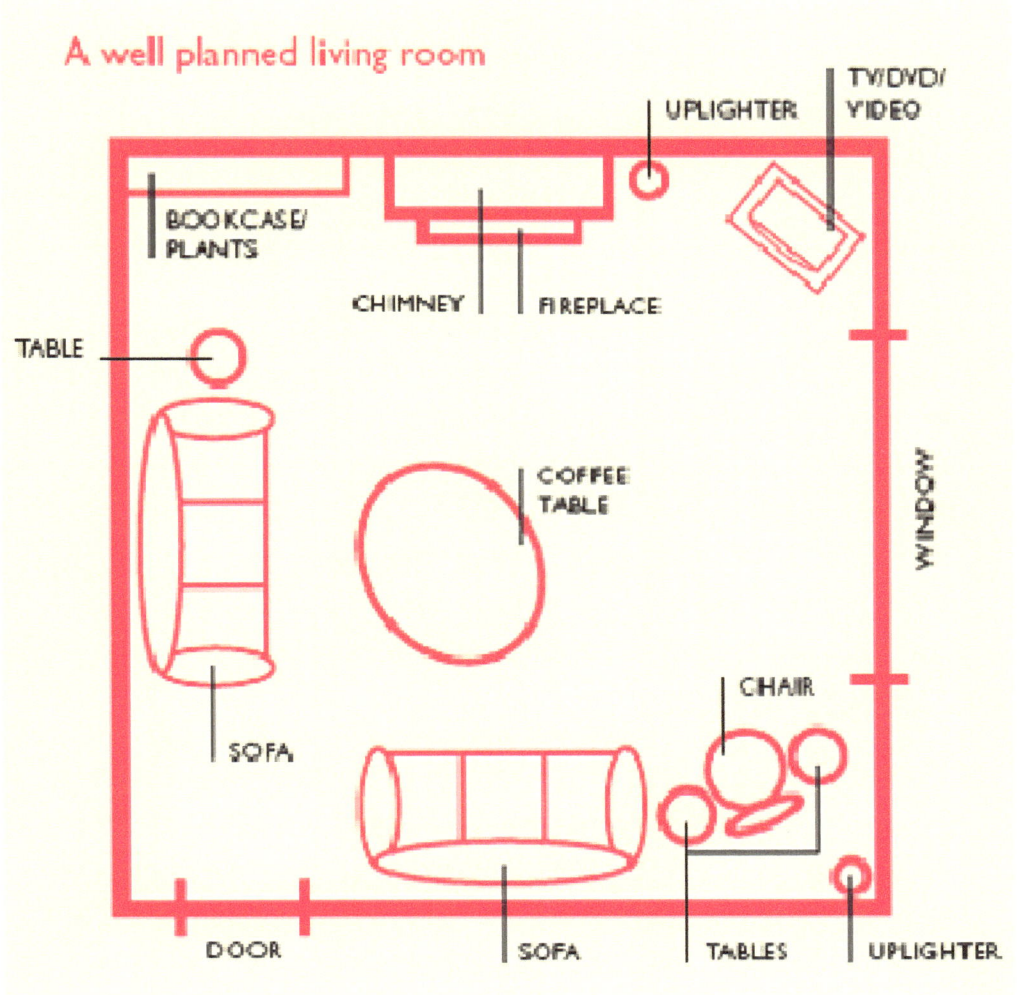

A well planned living room

TV/DVD/ VIDEO

UPLIGHTER

BOOKCASE/ PLANTS

CHIMNEY

FIREPLACE

TABLE

COFFEE TABLE

WINDOW

CHAIR

SOFA

DOOR

SOFA

TABLES

UPLIGHTER

Since the living room is the area in the home where you receive and welcome guests, the first instinct you have for it is to make sure that it is as presentable as possible-- meaning there are lots of natural light and it is clutter-free. But how about bringing positive energy? What if you can do that using simple tweaks in furniture arrangement and adding certain, simple elements?

The following are Feng Shui tips that are very much doable, and also very much effective:

1. A timepiece or clock should always be there.

More than just telling time, clocks in Feng Shui have ability to keep you safe. Experts say that you should surround a simple wall clock with bigger picture frames, preferably pictures of mentors, friends and family. If your clock has a pendulum, place it in the northwest section of the house-- more than just serving its aesthetic purpose, the clock will keep you safe when you travel if arranged as advised.

2. Lush plants

Plants signify vitality and life. If you have it in your living room, then you'll be getting more than just a breath of fresh air. Place a couple of plants in the southeast portion of the living room, for it is known to increase your chances of being wealthy. If you want to be recognized or be famous for what you are doing, then place some in the south portion of the area. The lush color of the plants also signifies good health, perfect for family members suffering from illnesses.

3. Furniture

Because TV symbolically attracts your focus and leads you away from the goals you have in mind, Feng Shui experts suggest that they should never be a focal point in the living room. As much as possible, purchase a cabinet that can hide the television from your view, if you don't want to buys one, place it in a diagonal direction.

This action will bring back your focus in your priorities.

4. The Fireplace

Since the fireplaces make the house warmer, it can help bring back the spark in the romance, especially if the marriage or the relationship is on the rocks. If your fireplace is on the south side of the room, it can bring you good luck in your wealth and abundance. If it is in the northeast, then you can expect to be more clear headed, thus, ensuring that you make sound decisions. The latter is also good if you are still studying.

5. Depictions

When it comes to pictures, you have to be extremely cautious.

Feng Shui experts reiterate the importance of picking pictures the depict happiness. If your photos are sad or violent, never place them in your living room. Same with romance, if you are single, avoid having a photo where you are alone, especially if what you are doing is staring out in space. Abstract art should also be avoided as they bring havoc in your life.

Solid pictures of family should be encased in a metal frame, signifying a very strong bond. It should also be placed in the west side of the living room. Doing so will bring the family good luck.

6. Mirrors

The rules in designing using mirrors are simple. First is that it should never reflect anything that's ugly, like a pile of junk. As much as possible, locate it in a place where the reflection shows abundance (food in the dining table), or flow of energy (lush plants, or river).

Another warning when it comes to mirrors, make sure that if it reflects the tallest member, the head is not cut off.

The Bedroom

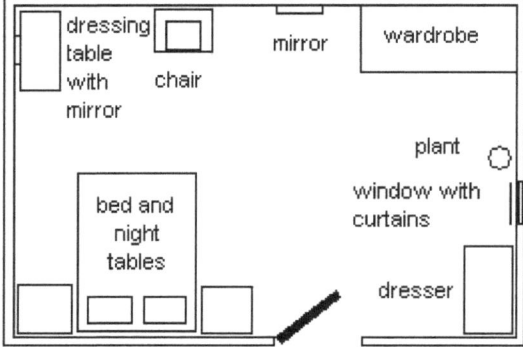

The bedroom is the center of romance. Experts say that of all the parts in the house, the bedroom is the easiest to manage because the techniques are very simple, logical, and doable.

1. Ventilation

It is important to have fresh air in your room, so if you have windows, make sure to open them frequently. If windows are a problem, then purchase a quality air purifier. Adding fresh air using plants is not advisable if your bedroom is small, but if it s large enough, the plants should be placed far away from the bed.

2. Your lover, and your lover alone.

Make sure that there is nothing in your bedroom that will remind you of your past love, and make sure that your partner does the same. That's why experts suggest that when building a family, the bed must be new, so that no remnants of past love will be there.

3. Equality

When it comes to equality, Feng Shui experts say that both sides of the bed should be treated fairly. It should also be large enough so when you crawl on it, you do not climb over your lover. Both sides should also be easily accessible. When choosing or fixing a bed, the headboard must be sturdy-- signifying the support of the lovers to one another. If you are planning to place bedside lamps, make sure that both sides have it.

4. Romance in the evening

If in the morning it is advisable to open the windows wide, the night should have a sensual lighting, which means nothing too bright. The technique here is to add candles, or dim side lights. These lights will set the mood for a perfect love making. The shadows the dim lights will create offer seductive power that neither of you can resist.

5. Colors and Mirrors

You have to be careful when decorating with mirrors. According to Feng Shui specialists, it is not a good idea to place a mirror in front of the bed it's because you will likely attract a third person in the relationship. As for colors, choose the most soothing and at the same time, seductive. That color range from pink to light brown. Never place red as the dominant color, but you can add few touches of it all over the room.

6. Photos

As for images, make it so that the dominating photos that'll appear are pictures of you and your lover. Adding photos of the whole family will distract you and will only reduce the privacy of the love making.

7. The Buzz

The general rule in the bedroom designing is this: never put anything that will distract you from sleeping, resting, and making love. That includes everything from workout materials, paper works, and household bills! These tips also work in Feng Shui! So, if you want your bedroom to be an area where romance blossoms and attraction sparks, remove anything that can distract you!

The Kitchen

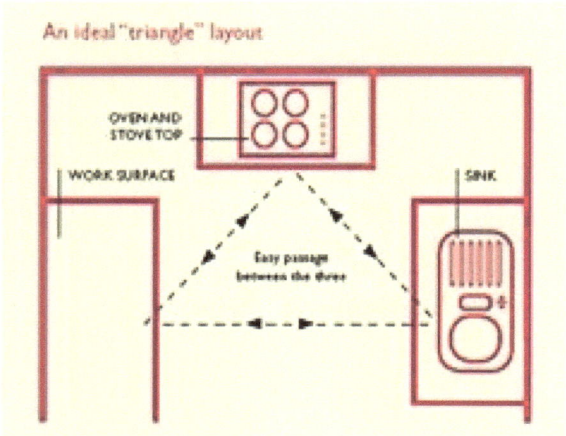

An ideal "triangle" layout

OVEN AND STOVE TOP

WORK SURFACE

SINK

Easy passage between the three

Gone are the days when kitchens are the exemption to style. At one point in our history, kitchens have to be clean (because this is where foods are prepared), but they do not have to be designed, much more, styled according to Feng Shui. But that is not the case today. If you want to have a Feng Shui perfect kitchen, which can nourish the life of the whole family, follow the tips below:

1. Standing your ground

Should you consider to seriously renovate your kitchen to make it Feng Shui perfect, make sure that you have earthen wares like potteries. If not, then ponder on turning your countertops into neutral tones. According to experts, the earthen elements or the neutral hues will keep you on your toes-- a requirement needed when you are handling volatile materials like knives and fire.

2. About gadgets

People with small space also often turn their kitchen into a dining area- experts have nothing against it, but they do have something to say when it comes to bringing in gadgets in the kitchen and dining room.

Feng Shui has it that the television, or any distracting gadget your have, should not be turned on while spending time preparing meals or eating. And no, that is not just because you are disrespecting the blessings, but more on distracting the good flow of communication that should be present within the family.

As much as possible, remove these distractions, or, if the space won't allow it, have it turned off during meal preparation and eating.

3. The glory of the chef

Feng Shui also suggests that the kitchen should always contain a happy and empowered cook. And no, it does not mean you have to purchase a statue of some sort, rather, you have to make sure that the cook in your house (more often than not, the mother), is feeling happy and empowered when she is preparing the meals for the household.

For her to be happy, keep the place of meal preparation in the kitchen island, where the cook shall feel she is an important part of the family. For her to be empowered, she has to know what's happening around her even while she is cooking, that means she should be facing the door or the window.

If that is not the structure of your kitchen (meaning the cook's back is to the door), then you can compromise by installing mirrors. It will also help if the stove is always on a good, working condition.

4. Safety first

Knives should not be somewhere it could be easily reached by anyone. Fens's shui experts have it that the reason why you should keep them hidden is not just because of safety, but also because of the feeling of security it will give you. When a cook sees a lot of sharp objects hanging in the kitchen, she is bound to feel restless and agitated. If that happens, the food she prepares for the whole family will lack the luster and the energy.

5. Doubling the wealth and fortune

According to Feng Shui, the burners in the stove are great symbols of prosperity and fortune doubling their numbers will also double your wealth and fortune. A simple mirror will do the trick. Just place a mirror above the burners, or even on the hood, and make sure the burners are reflected on it. When you see eight stoves instead of just four, then you have created the trick right.

6. Leaky faucets

As we have mentioned earlier, the kitchen is the area in the house where the whole family is nourished and the energy flows. Thus, it has something to do not just with the wealth and health, but also with emotions.

If your faucets are always leaking, be certain to have them fixed immediately. Feng Shui experts reiterate that leaking will drain not just the wealth of the household, but also the energy of the whole family.

7. Adding space

Since the kitchen is the center of the health and wealth, making it huge is a good action. This is sometimes the most frustrating problem for a household residing in an apartment area where the space is limited. Don't worry, though, experts said that you can compensate by making an illusion of a bigger space. Adding mirrors in the doors and making your kitchen as clutter-free as possible are the two best ways to add space to your kitchen.

8. Revitalize

Revitalizing your kitchen is very easy. All you have to do is to make sure that there are flowers and plants, in the area, or if you cannot afford to have those, then simply add fresh fruits in the table or countertops.

It is also important to fix lovely dinners in the kitchen at least twice a week. Due to busy schedules, all the family can manage now are quick meals and hurried eating. Feng Shui has it that the family should cook using their kitchen with love, at least twice a week. That means that the food should be intricate, with details, and should also be very tasty.

The Bathroom

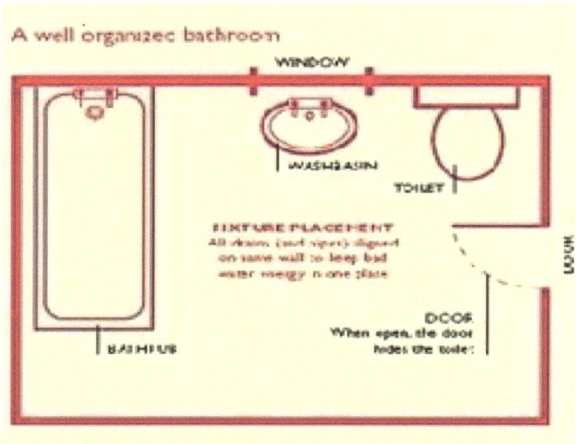

A well organized bathroom

The bathroom is a place where privacy is at its peak. Some homeowners don't even bother organizing their bathrooms because the family are the only ones using it. The only exemption is when guests are expected to arrive. However, Feng Shui experts reiterate on the need to pay attention to the bathroom because this is often the unluckiest place in the house. This is because the water is always draining from out of the toilet and tub.

The unluckiest position for a bathroom is in the south or north, because these are the areas of wealth and love. Having a bathroom in those areas mean the love and the wealth will also be flushed or drained out. But frankly speaking, your bathroom is already an unlucky area, regardless of the position. This makes Feng Shui even more necessary.

Relax. It does not mean that if your bathroom is in those two positions, you are doomed forever. You can counteract the effects by following the techniques below.

1. Soothing chimes

If your bathroom is located in the northeast or the southwest portion of the house, it is important to add metal wind chimes in the area. This is so you can dispel bad energy. Feng Shui experts also advised that when purchasing the wind chime, there should not be any Chinese symbol. The reason for the chime is to get rid of the bad energy, not to energize, so there is no need for symbols.

2. Crystals

If your bathroom is in the south portion of the house, you can dispel bad energy by placing crystals in the windows. The crystals will absorb the bad energy so your family will be okay.

The only problem in this solution is the cleansing of the crystals. Since they absorb too much of the house's bad energy, they should also be cleansed frequently. You can do the cleansing weekly or monthly and use methods such as moonlighting or burying them (the crystals) under the soil or herbs.

3. Plants

If your bathroom can be found on the north of the house, you can dispel bad energy by placing plants near the window. Doing so will not just freshen the air that you breathe, but it will also uplift your spirit.

4. Candles and Lamps

If your bathroom is located in the east side of the house, it is a good step to place candles or glitter lamps in the room. The fire in those accessories will dispel the bad energy. More than that, it will also create a good romantic ambiance and a soothing effect on a troubled mood.

5. Should your toilet be above the bedroom, kitchen or main door

Feng Shui professionals state that having a toilet directly above a bedroom, kitchen or main door is very unlucky. You can escape the unluckiness by having the light turned on in the bathroom for three hours straight everyday.

6. Stagnant water

Since the water in the toilet and bathroom is always being flushed or drained out, it is important to counteract it by placing water in an urn. This will ensure that energy and good luck will stay despite the flushing and draining.

NOTE: The elements we have provided above should not be placed anywhere where else other than the position we have mentioned. Example: do not place crystals if your bathroom is in the north portion of the house, and do not place plants if your bathroom is in the south portion of the house.

7. When using the bathroom, keep the doors open

But... be careful. If your bathroom is positioned near the kitchen, or in the bedroom where the bed can be spotted, or if the bathroom also faces another door... then always keep the door shut when using the bath. Otherwise, experts suggest that you should enjoy bathing with doors wide open (not always, especially if there are visitors or kids around).

The Home Office

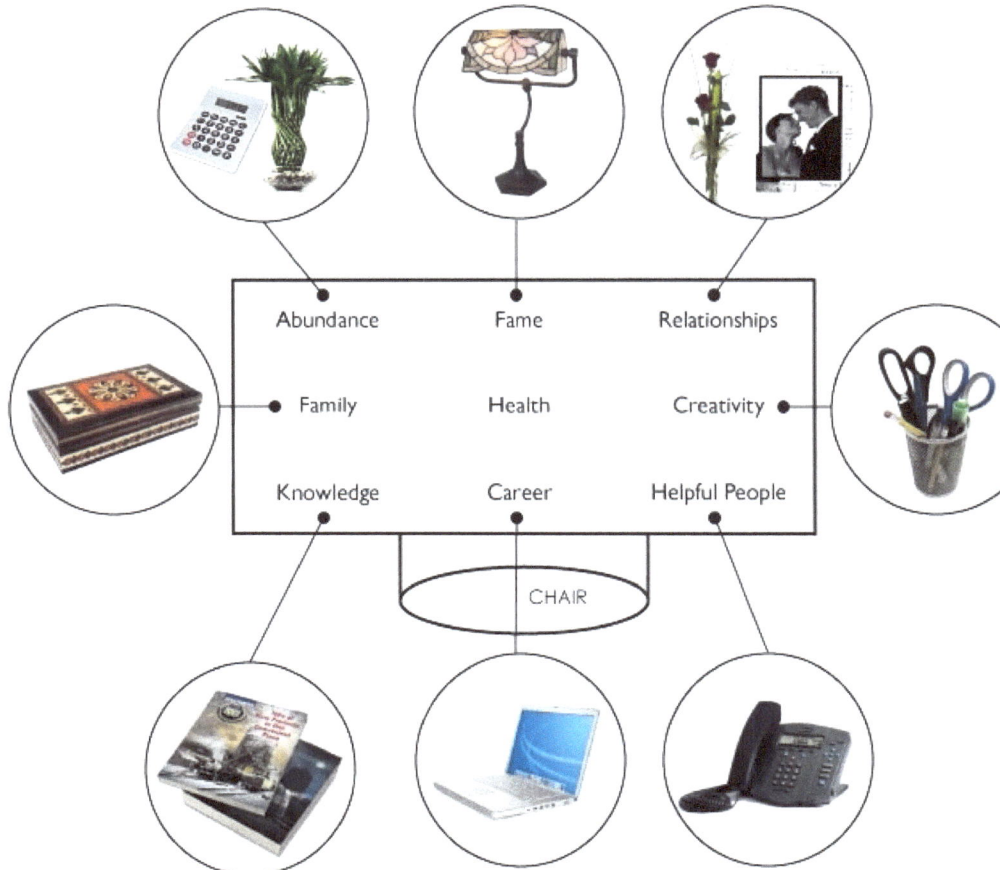

The home office is the place where most of your greatest ideas will be conceived. It is important that this particular area in the house is Feng Shui perfect.

1. The location

Unlike other area of the house, the home office is very flexible when it comes to location. So, before setting it up, make sure that it is nowhere near the bedroom because it can interfere with both sleep and romance. If you have a small space and cannot help it to set the home office in the bedroom, make sure that you install any form of partition, like a plywood divider or screen.

Avoid placing the home office in under the stairs because the area sis o cramped up and can interfere with idea formulation. The best place for a home office is a room with high ceiling-- which symbolizes lofty achievements for both career and business.

2. The power desk

The desk should always be brand new so as not to mix the ideas of the previous owner to that of yours. It should also be made of woods, glass desks are prone to breaking, and can symbolize the business deals and promotions to be broken too. Always choose a sturdy desk, never one where any of the parts are missing. To set you off in the correct direction, it is advised to not have anything under your table, especially trash cans.

3. Your position

As for your position, make sure that you are facing the doors (although not directly) and your sight can also cover the window. If your back is on the door, Feng Shui has it that there will be a lot of things going on in your back-- never good for any business or profession. Facing the door and seeing the windows will give you a tactical advantage.

When it comes to support and stability, make sure that your back is facing a solid wall, not the window pane.

4. Symbolisms

As for decorations and styles, it is advised for you to hang pictures or even quotes that depict the things that you want to accomplish in life. Images of family members are good because they act as support, but never have a lot of them because they can also cause distractions.

5. Separating personal life

Aside from making sure that your home office is as far away as possible to the bedroom, you must also take necessary steps to separate it from your personal life. You can do this by shutting the door each time you are there, or by creating a solid schedule. A ritual will also be a god idea- this ritual will prepare and command your mind that business is resuming. An example of a good business ritual is to light a candle or play some music before work.

That does not mean though that you cannot "include" your personality in the office. In fact, experts advise homeowners to design their offices with their own style and personality so as to cater the confidence and the comfort. After all, one cannot think well if the area he is currently in is not his own.

Conclusion

There are numerous mental and physical benefits to using feng shui in your life, and many of the practices outlined by feng shui are supported by scientific research. For instance, feng shui dictates that it is healthy to have living plants in your proximity. A study by Tina Bringslimark titled 'Psychological Benefits of Indoor Plants in Workplaces', found that individuals who had a plant near to them had increased productivity, reduced stress and better overall general health. Another study by Benjamin Poole saw student's attention span and learning motivations greatly increased after their classroom had been re-designed according to the principals of feng shui.

Don't be afraid to try different things. You do not have to be Chinese, or know anything about Chinese culture in order to embrace feng shui as part of your lifestyle. It can be incorporated into your surroundings and preferences. In fact, you should adapt the principles of feng shui to suit your lifestyle rather than trying to strictly adhere to traditional practices as this would not create harmony as it is designed.

This book is not intended as a comprehensive explanation of feng shui but rather an introduction to it. The information here has been simplified for ease of understanding, and due to space constraints. If you would like to learn more about feng shui and what it can do for you, consider consulting a feng shui expert.